SIMPLE ACTS OF KINDNESS
for Kids

by
Ray Alonzo

Simple Acts of Kindness for Kids
ISBN 1-57757-765-5
Copyright © 2000 by Ray Alonzo
P.O. Box 888
Fresno, CA 93714-0888

Published by Trade Life Books
P.O. Box 55325
Tulsa, OK 74155

A Note to Parents

This little portable guide, written for the young and tender of heart, is designed to help teach children compassion and the abundance of life through kindness toward others.

Read this book along with your children and volunteer to help them accomplish their good deeds. Encourage them with these creative, easy, and practical suggestions. Help them discover the rewarding and tremendous blessing of giving.

One life at a time—that's how we can make a difference. What better way to begin than through the heart and hope of a child.

Dedication

I dedicate this special book to my nieces and nephews:

Ali, Allan, Anthony, Christopher, Faith, Geoff, Jesse, Lori, Royce, Scott, Taryn, Wade
. . . and one on the way.

Acknowledgments

Special thanks to Christopher, David, Jason, Jonathan, Paul,
Paulie, Peggy, Ricky, and Stephanie for their unconditional
love and support in making this book possible.

SIMPLE ACTS OF KINDNESS
for Kids

Little Ways to Make a Big Difference

Open the car door for your mom.

•♡•

Pick up the trash nearest to your classroom.

Hold the door open for
the people behind you.

Drop your extra change in a charitable can.

•♡•

Go beyond the call of duty by
doing extra chores around the house.

Offer to help a classmate
with homework.

Walk a younger child home from school.

·♡·

Thank your teacher for making
a big difference in your life.

Run errands for your teacher.

Offer to walk your neighbor's dog around the block.

•♡•

Tell your librarians that you appreciate their help.

Teach someone younger
to tie his or her shoelaces.

Offer to water the yard on Saturday morning.

•♡•

Surprise your mom and dad by washing the car.

Volunteer to wash
a neighbor's windows.

Encourage the game officials
for good calls at the ball game.

•♡•

Thank your coach after a game
or practice for a job well done.

Give your coach a big bag of sunflower seeds.

Share your coloring book with others.

•♡•

Leave a couple of quarters in the
change slot of a telephone booth.

Let the miniature golf players
behind you go ahead.

Watch the sunset with a friend.

·♡·

Offer to clean up an elderly neighbor's yard.

Shovel the snow off
your neighbor's driveway.

Put out some birdseed in the winter.

·♡·

Roll the shopping cart back where it belongs.

Help set the dinner table.

Put a quarter into someone's expired parking meter.

•♡•

Share your umbrella on a rainy day.

Redeem your aluminum cans
and donate the money to a charity.

Teach a friend how to ride a bike.

•♡•

Give last year's winter jacket to a homeless shelter.

Clean out your closet and
donate clothes you've outgrown
to the local Salvation Army.

Clip coupons for your parents.

•♡•

Pick up trash around the playground in your local park.

Leave a token in the arcade
change slot for the next person.

Help your friend with his or her paper route.

•♡•

Give your best friend a hug.

Introduce the new kid in school
to your friends and teachers.

Take out the garbage the night
before pickup without being asked.

·♡·

Offer to water your neighbors'
flowers while they are on vacation.

Make your teacher a
homemade bookmark.

for KIDS

Send a card or note of encouragement
to a friend without signing it.

•♡•

If your parents discover they've left
something behind, offer to jump
out of the car and get it.

Make a happy-face greeting card
for your teacher and
have everyone sign it.

Give your good seat to an elderly man or woman.

•♡•

Let someone in a hurry go ahead of you.

Pray with someone in need.

Split a pack of gum with a friend.

·♡·

Wash dishes for your parents without being asked.

Write a "Top Ten List," explaining why you like your best friend.

Always show respect to your parents,
especially in public places.

•♡•

Take a box of your old toys to a homeless shelter.

Place a small piece of wrapped
candy on your mom's pillow.

Share a short story with a friend.

•♡•

Feed a neighbor's dog for the weekend.

Offer to erase the board
for your teacher.

Be a best friend to someone new in your class.

·♡·

Carve a smiling pumpkin with a friend.

Rake leaves in your neighbor's yard.

Take an apple to your homeroom teacher.

•♡•

Vacuum for your parents without being asked.

Give your teacher a
keepsake picture frame.

Help pick up litter left in the school yard.

•♡•

Collect used magazines for the senior center.

Smile and thank your
school bus driver.

Give a classmate a brand new pencil.

•♡•

Surprise your mom with
something you made from class.

Share your lunch with someone
who forgot to bring one.

Bring in the morning newspaper for your parents.

•♡•

Rake the yard.

Make the bed for your brother
or sister one morning.

Read a bedtime story to your little brother or sister.

•♡•

Share your popcorn and candy
with friends at the movies.

Volunteer to take out the
garbage for an elderly neighbor.

Turn in items you find to the Lost and Found.

•♡•

Offer to help clean your friend's room.

Pull weeds out of the yard.

Invite your dad for a short bike ride.

•♡•

Encourage a friend who is sad.

Look for something good
in every person you meet.

Offer to help when you see
someone drop or spill something.

•♡•

Volunteer to say grace with your family before a meal.

Make a homemade Christmas
ornament for your grandma.

Set up a *free* lemonade stand.

•♡•

Put the game balls away after use.

Volunteer to mow a neighbor's
lawn without expecting
anything in return.

Throw away the lunch trash
someone else left on the table.

•♡•

Make a thank-you card for your mail carrier.

Offer to care for a neighbor's pet
while the owner is away on vacation.

Always make a special effort
to return items you borrow.

•♡•

Offer to help wrap Christmas presents.

Leave a candy bar in the
mailbox for your mail carrier.

Forgive your friends when they hurt your feelings.

•♡•

Write an encouraging letter to a community leader.

Collect cans and newspapers
for a local charity organization.

Become a pen pal to someone
in a less fortunate country.

Let someone go ahead of you at the drinking fountain.

Offer to fold the laundry.

Smile and wave at a police officer.

Share your french fries.

Help feed your baby
brother or sister.

Stick up for someone who is being teased.

·♡·

Tell a funny joke or riddle to a friend who is sad.

Memorize a poem and
recite it for your parents.

Offer to bring in the mail.

•♡•

Call and cheer up a sick friend with a funny joke.

Include someone who usually
gets left out, in an activity
with you and your friends.

Send a photo of yourself along with
a love note to your grandparents.

•♡•

Help someone younger plant a bean
seed window garden in paper cups!

Encourage your brothers and sisters
by saying nice things to them.

Offer to rub your dad's shoulders.

•♡•

Tell your friends that God loves them.

Write a surprise note to your dad listing
three things you think are great
about him and place it on his pillow.

Offer to help set up the tent when you go camping.

•♡•

Compliment your dad's cooking.

Make a special snack for
your brother or sister.

Surprise your doctor
with a funny greeting card.

•♡•

Give your mother a "Best Mom" award.

Offer to wash the
windshield of the car.

Give your mom a smile and a good-morning kiss.

•♡•

Offer to organize the kitchen junk drawer.

Rewind the video rentals
before returning them.

Ask your grandparents to tell
you stories about their childhood.

Make a list of what you like about
your teachers and give it to them.

Give your parents lots of hugs.

Send a postcard to a friend while on
vacation with your family.

Start a hobby with a friend or relative.

Take extra pencils for classmates
on the first day of school.

Surprise your mom with a love note
on the refrigerator door.

•♡•

Offer to make your parents' bed one morning.

Combine your money with
your brothers and sisters to pay for
dinner out with your parents.

Let your younger brother or sister have
first choice of TV programs.

•♡•

Offer the last piece of pizza to a friend.

Make a get-well card for
a sick friend and have
all your classmates sign it.

Offer to carry the groceries in from the car.

•♡•

Make a date with Mom or Dad
to do something special.

Make juice pops for your friends
in the ice-cube trays on a hot day.

Offer to watch the stars with
your grandma or grandpa.

•♡•

Share your blanket while
watching TV with a friend.

Post a surprise love note to your parents on their bathroom mirror.

Volunteer to help your parents
with the map on road trips.

•♡•

Pray for your family every day.

Draw a colorful picture
for your principal.

Offer to use your allowance when
shopping with your parents.

·♡·

Introduce your parents to your
teachers on open-house night.

Plant a sunflower in the
backyard for the birds to eat.

Surprise your dentist with a big smile and a funny card.

Make some homemade Christmas
presents for your parents.

Take a morning snack to the
bus stop for your friends.

Bring your toys and other items in from the car.

Call and sing "Happy Birthday"
for your grandma or grandpa.

Bring your dad a cool drink
when he comes home from work.

Note from the Author

My one great motivation in life is to see a chain reaction of kindness explode around the world—one person at a time. What better way to begin than by teaching our children the abundance of life through kindness.

If this book has inspired you or if you have a few unique ideas to share, I'd love to hear from you.

Ray Alonzo
The Barnabas Group
P.O. Box 888
Fresno, CA 93714-0888

If you have enjoyed this book, or if it has
impacted your life, we would like to hear from you, too!

Please contact us at:

Trade Life Publishers
Department E
P.O. Box 55325
Tulsa, Oklahoma 74155

Additional copies of this book and other titles
in this series are available from your local bookstore

Simple Acts of Kindness

Trade Life Books
Tulsa, Oklahoma